C000052198

LIVE DEPICTION

Poems of Current Times

Reema Kumar

BlueRose
Publishers

First Published in September 2020

ISBN: 978-93-90380-71-8

BLUEROSE PUBLISHERS
www.bluerosepublishers.com
info@bluerosepublishers.com
+91 8882 898 898

Cover Design:
Priyanshi Shukla

Typographic Design:
Saurabh Yadav

Distributed by: BlueRose, Amazon, Flipkart, Shopclues

FOR THE FIRST READER

PREFACE

"Live Depiction" is a portrayal of the restlessness of the events occurring around. Words which were silent got a passionate voice. I found in my head a converter of visuals into poems. Reflecting tussie-mussie in the guise of poetry, the language of floriography. And suddenly I observed that my brain is fertile enough to grow more and more of it. Everything is going on live and rhythmic in my poems. As the name itself suggests they are the live sketches of the present times. Each poem has its own subject matter and an event. This book decodes my version of seeing towards the day today happenings, blunders and beauty. Subtle yet obvious. Visible, colourful and vibrant for those who want see and there is nothing to offer those people who are still, stagnant, unethical and non-flexible.

The key subjects that have been the focal points are the media, news, youths, intellectuals, system, democracy, earth, nature, polity, citizen, Gandhi, Nehru, Love, power, literature, life. Rather beyond life. And this list is incomplete. To get the whole of it, you need to capture the entire book. The display of the current issues and at the same time the sketch of the brilliance who tried to raise the voice for the sensitisation of the society. Heeding about the path we choose. I could easily sense the symbiotic relationship between the two.

Moreover, apart from so many subjects I also tried to give aesthetic attire to polemics which resulted in poetic form of art, radiating the real-life sequences. All of them are in different formats, sizes, shapes, free verse, herd etc. All in one, the source is that passionate spring which comes from the other side of the heart. To be true, my concern is also to celebrate and search my own self, my individuality, my personality by this way. I understand we all need certain corrections in our input, output systems to be more awaken.

I must thank to all the souls of eighteenth and nineteenth century poets who left back the craft of this philosophical art on the earth before physically leaving the place. Of course, I too smelled the aroma of those white yellowish pages which can fail the smell of any big brand perfumes. I gratefully acknowledge my inner voice for encouraging and keeping my spirits up. And inspiring me to read, learn and love knowledge

Typically, the core intention of my poems are to make everyone more live and perceptive. Obviously, theme is purely Indic thus I yearn Indians should read it. I hope the bluntness of the message of the book will certainly wake up the sleeping thoughts of the human brains. I do not belong to any literary cycle, rather I will describe myself as a "Beholding Recliner". And book is like a needle of watch that has captured the time. I welcome you all to this paradise of art which will make a pleasant knock on the ears passing a firm message to the mind of the readers.

Reema Kumar

New Delhi, 2020

CONTENTS

PHOTOGRAPH

You are a photograph
Your light falls on sensitive eyes
And the shape that occurs blends with vision
Now one can see the world in an extended dimension;

You are a picture
That nobody can ever blur
It has not taken by camera
It's an ocean of observation that has true colours;

You are an image
That comprises visual perception
So as words, idioms & collocation
You may be named as metaphor
To which William Shakespeare adore;

You are a reflection
That actualize waves and echoes
Flash in a form of pathos

An interface between the public and the administration
Which acts like a chewing gum composition;

You are a mirror
You show how naked we are
From inside out
Giving a chance to correct our fall out
By transferring manifestation not by means of predictions
But through serious deliberations!

———————— •★• ————————

TO A WRITER

Do you know?

You are a tree!

I'm scripting your inner look

After pondering in your mind

You yourself sowed the seed of yourself

To get a fresh peek

You germinated, you grew

In the organic matter called soil

As a living particle made up of 99% of atoms

About this I do not have a clue

I am only stating 1% of you;

Your sharp pen and set of opinions

May not always align with the readers

Or sometimes with the bosses of your publishers

Yet your roles are trailblazing, pioneering, ground-

breaking

Your quip have the power to enlighten the darkest tunnel
Your verses are full of weapons
Not your hands;

Your messages are simple....
That always feel you exist as an original
That feed your own soul
Through walking on an untrodden road
That too with the cluster of your thoughts
Before system chew up your roots
Analyse the culture
Throw away the vulgar
Oppose more, surrender less
At least practice your bit
Whether more or less
It's not only the work of the press;

And when done with whole day of scroll
Listen to the music of your choice
It can be Lata, Madonna, Amonkar, Lennon, Jackson,
Dylan ....
Before saying Good Night to troll!

———————— • ★ • ————————

REAL STYLE

Consistent and insistent is his style

His questions are simple but in piles

Nothing to do with one king!

Eight pawns, two rooks, two knights, two bishops, one

queen!

Which travels on 8 into 8 grid, miles and miles!

He doesn't play chess games

Where most of them resigns

Before the checkmating out of fear and hopeless fooling

lines;

His splendour eyes creates following words ....

"Self - Deception" is a new term

Thrown by the clown

New history is in making

Of taking steps without thinking

Against the clear thoughts

Where seeds never sprouts;

Carrying papers in one hand

He congratulates those who slept

But with comas and obliques tells all -

This sleep was to wake up again and stand

Wearing a jocund band!

On hearing this-

Sound occurs of enthusiastic claps

With an assurance to stand against the odds via protests;

Gathering the papers, he sum up –

This is neither a plea nor a prayer

One has to turn the layers

To find what's going wrong on the stairs of

the establishment

Also, on the chairs;

He /His! stands for a character

He /His! Stands for a badge

Of legitimate words

A vogue language to taste!

———————— • ★ • ————————

PROMPTER

I have a prompter

Who reads and writes for me

It gives me cue

My thoughts blew

Sometimes horizontal, sometimes vertical

It's all directions are mine

I uphold my goal

And start doing rock & roll

It's wise words dissolves pain

Leaving loneliness in vain

That is enough to keep me alive

Triumph is it's

I feel pride

I echo what it displays

Just like a mediocre person I grab solace

Feel as if I'm eating almonds

Sitting on a hill

Spell bound merging in thrill

It isn't a device

Inside me it resides

Whole year it naturally forms the sphere

Holding all the air of my heart

With it my day starts

After all, I have a "Prompter"!

———————— • ★ • ————————

ON - SCREEN

Ha Ha! Youths are getting patronage of unemployment,

poor education system and communalism,

They are right hand of this ism,

No scale is made yet to register it's extent

Whether they are moving forward or getting bent;

Selfies are today's best friend

And don't mistake it for trend,

Praise nature for its nakedness

And is defeating us in wickedness,

If we play with it Master Master

Then ecosystems may preach us via disasters;

Common love!

Let us be foes!

To our own girl child embryos,

We should go to Dubai

To say byegone to pretty,

Our love game shall remain toy

If we didn't get a boy,

Great! What a slogan we have got

"Save the daughter, Educate the daughter"

This is the one for which we vote wearing laughter;

Intellectuals have slapped with treason

Without any thoughtful reason,

Cowardice is becoming the power

Not ready to face meaningful words shower,

Press has become cafeteria

Hey! Have a coffee in an engraved cup!

Advertising the name of hub,

But we will not speak for letter writers existing in an

abandoned state of mess,

Who oppose such patriotism against his highness;

Would be laureates are free to talk against trees vs. metro reels

Wow! They are taller than the philosophical and scholarly ideals,

So! Cut the jungles!

In the midnight robustness;

After all we are UN wanderers!

———————— • ★ • ————————

PICTURE IMPERFECT

Are we all non-violent?

I don't think so!
So many people lynched in the name of show
Culprits behave similar to carrion eater befit in the family
of crow
Religion is not a sober word anymore
It digs your sore in the disguise of holy robe
Leaving you to cry in pain
You can't even enjoy rains
People are losing grip of the thread of hope
And this is not a drama or soap
Reality bites!
Just like mosquitoes as well as flies;

Gandhi is a road
One has to come in a walking mode
Picture perfect takes time

Patience added with colours of voices, books, a few steps

of agitation, composed looks

Are the ingredients when combines produce karmic node;

Driving smoothly is not an easy job

Driver is supposed to clear his brain fog

Of left & right-wing smog

Neutral space is required to come out of the wire

Switch on the music of desire

And put the seat on fire

Not to become mahatma

Firmly clean your "Atma"

And take your car to another rhythmical shore!

———————— • ★ • ————————

ERUDITION

Firstly, my bliss sat on plane

Then roamed in SUV on highways

Thereafter walked wearing slippers

In the gullies crossed the garbage litters

Though it's feet was in chains

Still walked to find the real stains

Of those filled in fears

That power smears

And throws just like frow

That can cut you before you grow;

I am counting the nuances

Of four years of advantages

That I gained in a lottery

Eventually turned into poetry

Got to know about communalism

How its undercurrent sprung

And flocked as if mushrooming drums

Furthermore, risks of rightness

Successes aren't only bed of roses

It comes in package that have clauses
Moreover, learnt about wording, lexicon
plus, word terminology
But remained weak in biology;

One more thing I need to say
Yup! I nourished stories in my brain
Boarded the creative train
Coached myself to come out of stupidity
In the form of vanity;

There is one special train
Coming up in some more days
Exact when I don't know
Sometimes, I chew up my jaw
Divine plan is under construction
To save me from destruction
For the better nourishment of my veins
To pull me out of strains
I just crave for brightness
After locked in inkiness
Neither being futuristic
Nor being pessimistic!
Amen!

— • ★ • —

TWO MORE DEATHS

What does this municipal do?

They can't even fix the sewers and manholes that overflow

Men are dying clearing the chocked lines

Workers enter inside without masks

No equipments supplied to them to do the dirty tasks

Soaked up in human excreta they swing up and down

When one gasps for air another one takes the chair

Takes out his undershirt

Tries to pull the hands of cohort

Oh no! He is gone!

Towards God's throne

He has left this hell for comfort zone

Nitrogen Oxides, methane, carbon monoxide, ammonia, hydrogen sulphide

Already took stride in his oxygen pipe

He is no more!

Second ones murmured voice flung up

Hey! I am too slipping down

Send me the rope

Stretch me out I have no hope

I am feeling asphyxiated

I can't cope

Politico did not take note until two dead bodies kept on
the road

Pain of families were grievous

Act of the government is heinous

Mr. Wilson fought back

Demonstrated against the loose ends of the Scavenging
Prohibition Act

TV channels are on mute mode

They have surrendered their remotes

A few are left by chance

Out of them one took that as an instance

To show the scene at a glance

But nothing much happened on our soil

Though international committee noticed the turmoil

Such voices received bow

For the issues like this they tow

At home front movie is same

No need to change the channel

Everywhere is same-same!

———————— • ★ • ————————

SOME MORE

Watch, they are coming back

Out of fear in slow pace

Struggling from HACE (High-altitude cerebral adema)

Climbing the stair

Sniffing the element of air

Which is accumulated in the sphere

Voices are returning

Complaining and murmuring

Traveling towards the dawn

Now one can see!

They are half roused

Marching to reach realm

Yet, they need to gather some more strength

Those voters who are awakened!

—— • ★ • ——

LET - OFF

Dogs can live without milk even on bread

Cows can too remain alive on pavement in the absence of green grass land

Children shall play indoors if there is no ground for hula-hoop game

We can too enjoy weather with no showers only rain bands

People may spend nights in huts

Minus castles build on islands

Boats will take you across the sea in the paucity of planes

Churches and temples can do in dearth of bishops and saints

In lack of gunpowder troops could manage battles with splashing ceasefire paints

So So So So...........

You can't imagine democracy

in the absence of fair media brains

And journalists can't perform without being true to the
ethics of their traits

No na!

Thus, clear the pollution in the communications

Before freeing the air from the chemicalisation

Release the stress!

Let - off the press!

From owners right!

For the survival of might!

In the favour of human rights!

———————— •★• ————————

REVENGE

Earth is taking revenge

Like an egg frying in a pan

Spirit of dead ones are crying

Asking for human body namesakes

One time more to correct the mistakes

O God!

Allow us to give another re-take!

Send us back on the cinema screen

We want to save the rickshaw puller

Struggling with a flood stream

He is weeping to save his livelihood

Lives are getting cheaper than the hood

Videos of despair are traveling to brook

Obviously on Facebook

Likes with comments are wavering, hesitating, irritating

Likers are confused which way to go

Blame game swinging to and fro

For Bihar & UP in a row

There is a catch here! You can wait to go!

Either Banglore or Chandigarh or anywhere in the globe

Your sweat is your power!

Anywhere you can throw!

Without thinking twice

Simultaneously feeling very nice

Just as politician bros

With confidence in a balance

As if you will be getting soon a heavenly abode!

———————— •★• ————————

PATRIOTIC SPIRIT

An honest man met an honest man -

An old man sitting under the rack

A young man noticed that track

He shook hands with him

His shrunk skin mixed with strengthen rind

150th Birth Anniversary of Gandhiji is nearing

Patriotic spirit is gearing

Somebody landed on the soil back home

Another one is gazing hand woven shawl allowing eyes to
roam

Gandhi's House is always full with bottles

Honey, soaps, shampoos, clothes

as well as organic juices without hassles

Old vs New

Story is little phew!

Old man wifey suddenly arrived in the picture

With a question that can puncture!

Why it is difficult to be true?

O Gentleman do you have any clue?
Tall man smiled carrying on lips a whew
Soberly uttered you both look same!
Both replied- yeah, we left that game of fame
It wasn't easy to survive in that line
Thus, we decided to live in decline
Soon two became three!
Blooming like they are on a celebrating spree!
All were wearing spectacles to see
Much cleaner and clearer air
And in a very simple atmosphere
Young man was typing minute facts
On his memory in a crispy format
He noticed there bucket is half full
Only things that were necessary to pull
Man and woman doing this together
Such stories are rare
Yet you can find them anywhere;

Yeah, I have got one
Clinched in my thumb!
Anybody can search to get some
Though such encounters are one in tons!

———— •✦• ————

MISSING PICTURES

September is close to an end
Started with awards ceremonies
Now speeches in UN are on trend
Everybody have their own explication
World is a book made up of words
Looks like a wrapped-up dissertation;

Rape victim pushed in stockade
So called culprit saint lying in hospital bed
Charges against him are severe
Luckily, he is close to the superior;

Two pictures running simultaneously
One on the hoard!
Other one on is the road!
Traffic jams, pollution & rat race
Real pictures are missing
Only flashes a single face;
"Are we the last generation"! "Save Aravali"!
"Save the Earth"!

"What a nice way to die"!

These are the posters

Children carrying on streets

They all want to get married

Thinking of playing with their grand kids

To become grandma, grandpa

Hip, Hop, Hap.........

Demanding the system to fail climate change on the map;

So many kids died due to oxygen supply lapse

It was one of the biggest mishaps

Countless such similar allegations

Hospital came under investigation

Paediatrician with beard shoved in jail

For nine months no grant of bail

Government pretend they did not misfire

Just fulfilled the people's desire

Now court has cleared doctor's name

Who will write back his wiped fame?

Wait until Monday

Tomorrow is Saturday and then Sunday!

———— • ★ • ————

370!

The Government says to the country-
Normalcy is back
You all can check on Twitter and Hashtags
Police chief was there!
And acknowledged there was no fear!

Article-370!
Now a history, moreover a mystery
Local politician kept out of sight
Locals are scared talking of human rights
Internet is still shut
Militarism walking on the ruts
Nowadays there nothing is a must;

The Girl complains to the media- Sir!
My name was on the merit list
I was unaware of this gist
You know the military's current mission
I have come here in adverse situations
I took the flight from Srinagar
After landing straight away I went to Jamia Nagar

To get the admission in JMI

But I was misbehaved

Labelled as stone pelter

My conscience thrashed

I was only there for admission

Advisor to the VC denied to grant such permission

Where should I go?

There are so many students in this row;

Real media raised the questions-

Why denial?

Why only they?

Quick answer is needed!

Why government is dumb & numb?

Or the girl is folly & grunk

But she has all the proofs

Speaking calmly not in huff

Kashmir is an internal matter of talk

Why on international rock?

Raising temperature of thermal clock

So many answers are required

Can you people stay at home

For four consecutive days?

How can they for 50 days?

Without any connection on hay!

———— • ★ • ————

POISON

We are two steps ahead of axis
Ready with atomic bombs and match boxes
Number of mortality encrypted in advance
Poisonous words have got all liberty to romance
Nobody can see that by chance;

Decoding machines are fired
Political supremacy features it's own desires
In the form of "Howdy" attire
Opposition is tied with the wire
Raids, jail, no bail!
No advocates are left for them to hire;

Give access within you to the information which is right
Political conspiracy may try to inject you fake light
They are pushing you to the suburbs from the cities
Where there is superficial hip-haps
Alkaline water runs in the taps
In summers electricity makes the place hell
One feel like drowning in the well;

People are wandering in a state of disillusionment
More distressed less content
Philosophy of politics is converting into circus
No questions only dancing lectures;

Circumstances are perplexing, troubling for both the
friends
Poetry and democracy cannot shake hands
Visionary thinking loosing its base
Is this a normal phase?
Where most of them are carrying fuel of hate!

———————— •★• ————————

LET ME AWAKE ALL!

Advocacy of polite literature

Should be the motto of the professor

They are the manufacturing unit of intellectualism

They mustn't sound like mum;

Formation of imbalance is going on

Oh! How citizens can accept destruction of minds?

O Boys Common!

Have you all lost your thinking capabilities?

Do you want to see your land in casualties?

Country is drifting apart from the truth

There is bacterium coccus spreading the myth

One should not forget.

That tongue crave for both sweet and salt

There are no such markets where there is only single mart;

This is not a lecture sort of stuff

Stand up to be little tough

Peace is nothing but a plain white paper

On which you can write sensible

Create a bright future

We don't need to rupture your language

To become a patronage;

Do not shout hoooohooooo!

Please don't clap!

Don't waste time in clicking snap

You all will miss the flight of road map

And this is not a joke

Do you all want your existence in havoc?

Love the people first than the earth

Gandhian land in on stake

Swedish Academy still regret

Why they didn't take stand on time?

To grace Gandhi with Nobel Peace Prize for his shine

Take a lesson from this line

Now bye bye!

Don't chuckle this is no witticism

Let me leave for another transaction;

Let me awake all!

Through my words!

That's my "Prime..." goal!

———————— • ★ • ————————

CHARMER

I am gaining the art from my charmer!

Practicing every day to save myself from any disaster

I look at his watch

Every day at any cost

I get the lessons in the form of roller coaster

Via gestures, voice and suggestions

He always leaves back impression

Indicating roots but no fashion

Like leaves of trees doesn't connect to sensation

Looking upwards!

Allowing chlorophyll to absorb the light of the sun

Thus, photosynthesis is done

As a result, earth receives fresh air

People wait so long for such glare

Through messages and chats

Where there is no race like rats

Existence of the soul is premiere

Dates of final results arrive

In a posture of thrive

Through his pressure not price

His mild touch brings smiles

On the wounds away miles & miles!

———————— • ★ • ————————

TABLE OF NEWS AT 9

Media is on a way of ending

Like a dead man on ventilator

Trending trending....

Every Hindi news channel has a same story

Of Indian strategies and Pak theories

I have made a table of news at 9

ABP throwing master stroke straight away claiming it
right

DD is confusing people through oil and mines

Aaj Tak taking audiences back to Rama's history

As if they are the real news factory

Zee has its own forensic lab

They test DNA

People call it Ah! So Fab!

India TV is sitting on LOC

They do not scare of bombing and screaming

News 24 is now presenting data of population

Crying inconsolably on dropping numbers of saffrons

Now comes NDTV India Prime Time screening

Talking about NRI's teaming, their very well streaming

Paid advertisements of government's projects through tendering

Along with candles students are marching

To save the university dying and lurching

Claiming Sanskrit is on the path of corrosion

Cases are pending in courts for proper pay scale

Again, here also visible erosion

Time to take a break ....

Cleaner are dying in septic tanks

Supreme Court has made strict comments

Nowhere in the world we see such lapses

Now what to say!

Report is ready anyone can access!

———————— • ★ • ————————

GANDHIAN SOLDIER

Parents will never allow their children to play with a lion

His teeth, jaws, nails frighten even the giant

So why not tell them to become a soldier

Which never fights with gun magazines

Rather gives everyone a thought to read

Free of cost laced with a language

In the form of numerous write ups

And one can play different roles

At the same time pantomime as a teacher, cobbler,

Barber, cook, sanitation worker, may be rickshaw puller

You can call them Gandhian soldiers

They will not only learn to honour the nation

So as the native tongue without hesitation

Tell them to grab the position on the globe

To fight battle of hope

Which they may win or may not

Though always be remembered that they fought

Soberly and gently being suave

In manners which are polished,

refined, noble and composed!

———————— •✦• ————————

CHAP BOOK

I have started writing a chapbook

For the tallest man once I have encountered

His unmistakable accent targeting deep into the heart

Was like an echoing in the mountains as well as on the
rocks

Talking about people in the margins

Struggling to cross political boundaries

I snapped his straightforwardness and vigour

To keep with me as an honour

I arrived in a blue, black and white attire

As if i was wrapped in a paper

Like a book to be inaugurated

My new life ready to be celebrated

In the intonation of his voice outside

A sea formed deep in me inside

Actually, it wasn't me

It was his posture reflecting in me

I was dumb

He lectured loud

I felt proud

Soon I came back

With a sack full of words and a map

To write a chapbook

Which I want him to read on my lap!

CLEAN THE ATMOSPHERE

Make the country wiser

Feed it with dark chocolate

Let citizens brain be less strained and much straight

Let it raise their HDL

Let it protect their LDL

Allow ORAC to absorb the free radicals from population

Yeah! I'm talking about liberation

Liberation of thoughts

Sovereignty in true sense

Not in people's absence

Voting shall not remain a finger gesture

Not only for people's pleasure

Democracy is much more than that

Of questioning the acts

Of government as well as political aristocrats

Such exercises can't be practiced in a gym

It's nothing sort of muscle showing in a rim

Nor it needs specific intellectualism

One need to exercise this in a day to day affairs

Just aim to protect the rights of individuals

"The Rule of Law" must be supreme

Where human rights may not only for creams

Free the atmosphere

From the air that stinks!

(ORAC - Oxygen Radical Absorbance Capacity)

———————— • ★ • ————————

FEAR OF LOCK

Nudity of wisdom is fair

Brings you all out of despair

Many exit doors in front

There are some in rears

People are still locked

In their own destructive spheres;

Say something say something

If nothing say I am here

I am here, still here

In the space of freedom

Make yourself thought less

For some moment

To recollect energy and submerge fear;

Sun may melt your bout

Snow may freeze your tout

Take pre cautions whilst going out

Never compromise in your shoe size

Always try to be a little wise

This is no fairy land

Everyone has to take their own stand;

And it is as simple as that!

————————— • ★ • —————————

LABELLING

Survey of the city is going on

Aim is to kick the plastic

Say it a bygone!

In real it is eying to save the throne

All the NGO's are crawling at the feet of the crown

O Superior!

See we are here along with our team

We too are in a row to protect your dream;

Plastic pollution is choking our ocean

For sure have to come in motion

It is poisoning communities, locations

Thus, needs immediate global solution

Before it sets eye on one more commotion

Which is rupturing our society

Hammering office table!

Sir! You are guessing well!

It is communalism in a form of hell

Can't we kick out both together?

In a subtle manner;

Calendar is ready for every occasion

There are some more things to mention

Gandhi jee is still a hot cake to vend

Can be labelled on every movement at the end

Take a instance on rent!

Quit India Movement

Quit Plastic Movement

What a match!

Just like one more feather in the hat;

Bapu's sayings are leaning on the racks

In libraries as well as in the study of literary

Why Gandhi jee has become so lonely?

After getting so many honours en awards

Why he is in melancholy?

May be his tall figure is getting hijacked by loathsome
theory!

———————— • ★ • ————————

ASK!

O youths chase the darkness with the voices

Ask the government -where are jobs?

Ask the question regarding GDP and crops

Tell them we don't feel good

We throb while mobbed

If one-person cry why not whole India should pay the
price?

Questions should come from the brains and strains

Ask –

why so much dirty are my trains?

Why don't you provide us free books?

In lieu of slogans that hang us on hooks

And why mafia grabs the land?

Leaving farmers alone on the sand

Tell them to solve the questions regarding EVM's

You have crossed the age of eighteen

Learn to speak your own brains minus refrains

Why don't you do physical protests

Speak, write and go on the streets

Not over Twitter and Hashtags

This should not to make requests but to submit facts

To protect the wetlands!

To restore the rivers!

Coz we are not meant to cross flooded lands

On canoes in fears

Not only India cleanse the whole Asia

Northern and Eastern hemisphere of earth One by One!

It's the mission worth

Act like an automatic washing machine

Clean and dry the country from within

Oh, youths lynching can never be right

In the name of religion and might

But be optimistic!

Alright!

At the end of the tunnel

There is always hope for the light

Put your points in very centric ways

To strengthen democracy with full grace

Oh, youths chase the bogus people out of the power and seats

Not the citizens who are struggling to live real beauties!

———— • ★ • ————

COSMOS

His brain represents cosmos

Glowing like light

Can clear the minds

Of the people sitting in the last lines

Yawning, half asleep, we can call them creepy

Recognitions travels to him in the platter

But not without effort

And not in the orchestration of platino (platinum) medal

His recognition has been awarded by angels

He does his actions with all the obligations

Remains true-blue in his course of actions

And waits for the white-collar reactions

Who are responsible for taking serious actions

In the standard in which democracy should perform

Yeah! the fourth pillar of the constitutional spinal cord

Journo, Anchor, writer & Broadcaster!

———— • ★ • ————

TIME PASSES BY

I roam around not to get bluff
Just to feel the puff
Of passion like stuff;

I waste so much time in waiting
For the unseen that is fading
My clothes are not like before
They badly need a wash at the shore;

I swim to get the touch
Of aqua!
And it's velvet punch
Grabbing my whole
As if superlative clutch;

When the orange day ends
Darkness calls!
Rings the bell in the manner
Egyptians scrolls;

I wave in the night to my might

Before closing the doors

Of my lashes under the brows

Then I get lost in the frost

To see the other day

I also sense dew kissing a leaf far away;

Time is leading a few hours ahead

Festivities beneath shed

I can't grab the watch

Thus, I'm sitting here downward back

Having my own swatch;

Here I'm feasting every moment in a leeway

That can stay with me in a form of clay

In my roots to smell my way!

———————— · ★ · ————————

BLACK - OUT

So many colours and so many scenes on the screen

For so many years we were watching

But we could hardly see any words nor any stories

All of a sudden there was a black out

Just like during period of wars

Visible changed into invisible

Only words left

And the thorough facts

And a cultivating voice

Carrying invoice

Rustle bustle was the sound

Everywhere in the next round

That was the "Holy Spirit"

Crossed it's limit

Introducing us to the sage

People who were in rage

Calming us down

Gifting us crown

Once more take us to black out

Where dusky means gleaming

Where veins starts reasoning

We wish to cheer so loud

For the simple reason

We are proud of that black out !

———————— • ★ • ————————

TOTAL COLLAPSE

Can we write a new chapter?

Can we hire a new teacher?

But the teacher is in wire!

How can we fulfil our desire?

No reflection of realities in the daily news papers

In Hindi not at all

In English there are some but miserable fall;

Nectar of information is no more required

If happens so editor shall be fired

Can we create renaissance?

Where no explosion of words are in essence

To spread fragrance,

Dozens of meetings takes place

Comes out what ?

Zero symbol of impact;

Equilibrium of thoughts are collapsing

Perfect is the time to do sonneting

Yet missing!

I am enveloping this genes

To gather the scattered appearing verses

Which may sound symbolism

Though not sure of any such phenomenon;

Actual is turning into history

And history has become mystery

Please keep on worshiping the leaders!

In temples their idols could be practicably fitted

This is the one enduring thing we created;

Congrats citizens!

For this unfading vision!

———————— • ✦ • ————————

POOR SPOKESPERSON!

Free us we want to run away

Towards the bay

So that we may speak in our own way;

Don't cage us!

Don't stop us!

Our vocal chords are still good

We crave to remove our hood;

Other side is literate

We should go there to concentrate

On the topics of current scenario

To put serious submissions

To talk with assertions;

All the time we miss that space

Of expression and grace

Where all colours become one

No difference between saffron, green, plum and golden

Where discussion flashes rainbows

Turning the hoarse into mellows;

Free us we want to run away!

Towards the bay!

———————— •★• ————————

PERSONA

New type of tangible persona he holds

His stunning success unfolds a lot more than gold;

The questionnaires, wires, desires of the people he represents

In the phases knocks the power with competence;

He never celebrated maths

Like mostly advocates

Rather choses his own ways

In line with attendance

To the truth that finally dictates;

His frequent mentions, insistence for solitude

Are only to become more better, much performing institute

That itself expresses dazzling gratitude

For the priceless love he gets

Back from the populace

In form of resonate flute!

———————— • ★ • ————————

OPEN SHOP

His shop is open for everyone

There is no lock,no key to turn

He never shuns the crowd in despair

Always ready to give a try for repair

When the screen becomes dark

His voice spreads light

Whole intelligentsia welcomes this glaring insight

Except those whose brains are swollen and tight

That's not a transitory consciousness pouring in tons

Should be preserved for millions of years to come

In it's perpetual form of plum

Until human beings exist

Until House of Lords forms

Until peers of realm returns!

———————— • ★ • ————————

VISITOR

Suddenly a visitor tapped onto my inward door

I flung opened and found Lenore

Morning of eighth filled me in arms

Setting aside past decoding my charms

There was no raven to pass indications

That someone shall knock to make predictions

Marvelled month emersed like an aquatic plant

Converting my inner noises into a chant

Same circle of spell produces carols

Protecting my within from outer clamours!

———————— • ★ • ————————

FOUR IN ONE

1)

I do not exist anymore

I am lost in you

There is a rose in my garden

Although fragrance touches you;

2)

Meeting of Zeus and Terra deferred for a while

Yet rainbow blossoms

After rain dries;

3)

Everything is organised in a messy train

Plenty of strain in a lucky brain

Until reaches required destination;

4)

Every day we get up together

To gather some time

Then reap the weather

End up cultivating another season

Little more better

Having an effectual reason;

———————— • ★ • ————————

NO DIALOGUE

There is a face wrapped in the cloud

On & off peep to see the crowd

On the earth planet

To weigh it's pressure, gravity, density and radius

It's crushed beauty

Coz eyes have to do it's duty

Does that mean one can throttle if

someone is flawed?

So many impressions splash in the air

Unanswered unlike the theory of Sigmund Freud

No dialogue between the sick and the psychotherapist

Thus, totally wayward to detect the sound

Which one is subtle?

Which one is frowned?

———————— • ★ • ————————

PAIN OF LYRICS

Love arrived back

With hands full of gifts

In one hand meadow

In the other sarcastic surgery of stupidity

Superior degree of doctorate fix in sleeves

When boarded the air

Thee floated the sea

From the windows of fog and mist

Giving story a new twist

Fearless, unknown with longed gist

Transferring the feeling how chained people thinks

Black and red are the colours

Combination that thrills

To them who are dead

No blood flows in their skulls

But they can walk

They can talk

Faster than any other species

Switching back to Sunday's

Where boredom sings Songs of dreams

Pain of lyrics

Ting tong trims

Ding dong shrinks

Love arrived back

With eyes that swims

On every possible themes!

———————— • ★ • ————————

DRINK OF POWER

Drink of power put you in awe

One starts sailing in complete flaw

Face without agitation reflects soothe and soften glow

Monies can buy the numbers

Everything can come in your tumbler

Intoxicating you from within

Minus soul that wiggle upside down

Melatonin proves futile in keeping calm

Meticulously searching for self-realisation

That can pierce the frontalebone

Making exit for cool breeze

But in this circumstance, this is not the crease

Such soulful happenings doesn't come in sleaze

Hallucinate and meditate to get such taste

Before that stop running in the rat race

Become feeble en simultaneous surrender yourself in

solace

Spit the artificial to exist like ardent fate

Converting powerless into most substantial confidante!

———————— • ★ • ————————

PREPARATIONS

One can discern people from their tongue

Whether one loves "laddu" or maple syrup waffle

This way you can determine the border in the orb

Who reigns passion in the hub is the real

Genius and sagacious

Doesn't stay awake in the night to make love

In the moonlight that "one" prepare tough questions for
the sun

Derive meanings from vociferation

From the papers that roar beneath the table cover

In between mingle with the air

Spill fragrances minus fear

Through words which never put smear

And everyone can easily bear!

———————— • ★ • ————————

BLOG

When you are somebody you have a blog

For hours and hours you push yourself to slog

In public your theme paper is no less than to clog

Not from being simpatico but with an advisory not to weigh frog

Outside the heart attainment soars identical to shog

Making you jumpy in your dreamy throb

This is merely not the absolute picture of thou!

Multifold shades are still left to describe somehow

Instead let me enumerate the tasks of sea

Which resembles all the elements of eternity, benevolence,

modern en orthodox, prose en verse tied in one string

Flowing then and now

All the time doing real plough

In the barren brains to cultivate acumen bow!

PAPER AND PEN

I sit with paper and pen in the morning

Along with the rays which

comes in shining

My pen soaks in the ink

Making me pink

Paper becomes blank

When I shrink in my own arms

Creating a new tale for myself

Fresh, new and I phew

Unlike dew

Everlasting thoughts shimmer in my blood

Goosebumps throws me in the air

As if I am the lightest particle on this universe

Suddenly, I find myself converse

Registering all the drama on the earth

Having a point of myself

Fabricating a new world for my persona!

———————— • ★ • ————————

ANOTHER OCEAN

Ocean on the earth thrills

There is another that flows in my fibril

Sky shines bright high up there

And one is here deep inside gathered in my blue frills

Heaven about which people speaks but unseen

I possess one in my en route dreams

Enchanting fondle, lectures and speeches

I sense myself on lofty peak

Everyone please make guesses what kind of unaccustomed

breeze is this?

Liquefy and at the same moment freezes!

———————— • ★ • ————————

INCARNATION

There is no knowledge in the information
Bodies left the souls for incarnation,
Written words sounds alike silence
Speeches proves to be like violin
Full of rhythms with hardly any themes;

The street of hate is the ultimate fate
Pumped with pollution craving for oxygen,
But!
Mr Right is so happy!
Mr Left is so sleepy!
Mr combat is not peppy?
So what?
Well, polity adjusted very well on the cot!
"Mallapuram" shining on the top
Historic moments, one-hour meeting, dinner & eating,
Press is very well treating topics that are hot,

But no solutions for banks that were robbed

Left the clients aloof en shocked;

Invitation has been accepted by the ministry

To visit China, the peers country

Another trip in the making

News is breaking!

Not their heart for the encountered man

Who refused to pay off!

And fought back against policemen!

———————— • ★ • ————————

MANIFESTO

It's a real story not a tale

Dusk is darkest and twilight failed

Manifestos are not declarations

They are the files that reflects deteriorations

In the agendas!

Name them fundas!

Feast only in a rupee

No need for employment spree

Youngsters keep your mouths shut!

We will provide you all free huts

Shivaji Bhonsle was the only king

We are Marathas, we only believe in Hinduism

Learn to chant vedic coronation mantras

Take dips in the sacred waters of seven rivers -Yamuna,

Indus, Godavari, Narmada, Krishna, Kaveri and Ganga

Death and succession are the real missions

Meanwhile trying hand to fight in election

It's a place of divine and artistic blend

So, we take it as a trend,

We just need to ring a bell

Stars bow on our feet, comes out of their shell

Arrow and Bow when mixes with lotus

An alliance sparks!

Compromises between brothers is not a new

Unity is a must to get green grass

Not for cows as all have been moulded in brass

Farmers loans shall be waived off

As they are left with no clothes to take off

It's a new form of time!

We eat gold!

We cut! We keep in lockers! Pines what we call!

———————— • ★ • ————————

PROTEST

Gather crowd in the heart of the city
To protest against the power
That shrinks your kitty;

You can't stop living where unemployment at its highest
Side by side cinema hall seats at its fullest;

You have to survive where gap is widening
Between the people for their faith in religious teachings;
You cannot bypass the air saying breathing is lethal
Still, you walk, you talk, you eat, you work, you drive,
where pollution is at zenithal;

You may not escape the news flashing on the screen &
papers
However, you can rationalise your minds by
mooting with such advocators;
You may be unable to talk in front of the camera
But you should write down and throw your thoughts in
opera;

So, for this simple reason-

Gather crowd in the heart of the city

To protest against the power

That shrinks your kitty!

———— • ★ • ————

LOSS OF SIGHT AND INSIGHT

I have taken a fresh way to talk to you my readers

With you my relationship is the same but the art is new

I absorb your compulsion

And splash like an emulsion

I order you to take an opportunity to come up of air

Getting blind in a sighted world

That is not a chapter I prepare

You all can live minus eye sight

But not in fright

I provide you the breathing space

To free you from Hape and Hace

Where series of dying is taking place

Death of linguistic skills!

Death of egghead pills!

Death of rationalising that chills!

You are walking like a person who

suddenly loses sight

Blow completes when leave you immobilise

You are made to believe that you will fall

If you try to cross the wall

That the flooring is incomplete

That the railing is missing from the stairs shall give you fit

You are forced to face both situations

Neurotics plus real agitations

My appeal is to stop watching television

Because you have already lost your vision

First get back your sight

I am an ophthalmologist!

I suggest ....

Wash two pulpy things below brows of your eyes

And then read & write

You may get back both sight and insight!

———————— • ★ • ————————

I TRULY STATE....

I have written for you a verse

Not for them who curse

Only you can tell how it is like

But don't say this thing on mike

I can understand both your space and face

Why you are restless and when in solace

I pour all my adoration for you

Sometimes in yellow and sometimes in blue

I may not utter in the name of God

For sure I shall write

And drop you a postcard

Now that I don't have register to doodle

So, I am thinking of sending you everything I scribble;

Further I truly state ....

Well, today itself I have plagiarised your sermon

At the time of dawn

People are ready to jump in a fire of drought

Paucity of wisdom is now most sought!

Where moral has gone to play football

Inspite of good breeding and training

There is a bridge where culture is draining;

My personal collection of books is only your oration

The ventilation is your voice

Which transmits vibrations

That's all in this vessel

Wait for my next epistle!

Yeah, I am talking about Bengal!

———————— • ✦ • ————————

RATIO

Don't try to scale ratio

Because your mathematics is zero

That doesn't mean you aren't a hero

Calculate miles and direction through patience

The stuff that one gets in ration

Scattered thoughts!

Lonely whereabouts!

Compute everything in caution

High rise planning are blocking the air

And that's not fair

However, I know sky takes care

Yet at intervals heat waves comes

Which chokes my gulping pump

Waiting for the pulls to over ·

Between the road and the flyover

From where the green field starts

Amidst an easy chair swings

With a little girl like wings

I pray to God

For the corrosion to stop!

———————— • ★ • ————————

MOUTHPIECE

I wake up with a pristine mind
Soon after my search starts for satirical signs
To feed my brain cells
In order to make them divine;

I too collect pictures but not of fixtures
Neither I pluck the leaves from trees
Nor I sit on the chair in peace
I take everything from mouthpiece;

From here the poetry begins
Sometimes on electoral notes
Sometimes on impaired inhabitants
Present may become history
Or history may become index
By any chance can't we bring back the tenure of fax?
Not possible!
Relax!

I don't remember from where I began

O Wow! now it's reaching to an end

The governor must be banging his head

Which party to call to form the government

Unclear is getting clear

Now that opposition is coming out of fear!

———— • ★ • ————

WHEEL

Today

Time moved

on wheels

I tried to

Grab

But couldn't

So bought frills

of lights

From roadside

Hawker

To hang

But couldn't

I am not that

Lofty

My hands

Are

Scanty

Will try again

Not in

Any frame

It's a puzzling

Festival

Slips from my

Hands

As soon as I

Try to

Hold

Tight in my soul

You people take

It all

I am here good

In my hall

Of solitude

Will burn the fuel

of my thoughts

To recreate

Disposition!

———— • ✦ • ————

SATIRE

Didactic is his voice

Fourth estate not a noise

Call him satirist

He too deliver natural instincts

People call him genius

Though sometimes gets comic

When he is serious

Seeing is his passion

Writes in a fashion

These are the characteristics which one can scan

Beyond this there is so much under sand;

You are mistaken!

I am mentioning about seven seas in one land

Relaxed, casual, spontaneous

Are the waves

Passes amongst lines

Actually, where he most shines

To people in the conference hall

Through his vocal cord;

Again, you all mistaken!

I am telling about Ocean

Multiple dimensional details where comes in motion

Pulls most of us out of notion

Salty or sweet

But never in haste

Suggest us to release

Teaches us to be little slow

When everything is in flow;

Please don't be mistaken!

This is about deep blue lagoon

In a craft of colloquial moon

It takes not less than 300,000 years

To come in formation

A single piece

Of own style

An era

I am the luckiest to gather everything it wipes;

This is about a man from noble clan!

———————— • ★ • ————————

CLASSICAL VERSE

Put classical attack on the authority that hunt
Is the best way to vent
Demonetisation was like a shot on the pulse
As if sneak thief has snatched your purse;

Leaders are playing upon theology
Struggling to survive is the literature
Subjects left to practice is history, and psychology
O, let's take a midway
And talk about biology;

So, what if ....
The literary influence of academies are fading
Chill and thrill!
Nothing is happening close to shocking;
Don't bring all subjects under scrutiny
Rather dance alike Britney!
Such orders are not on the paper
You only need to understand
The language of rapper;

I submit....

Poetry should replace the religion

To console our intellectual fusion

Journalistic skills are of no use

Minds of the editors are confused

Give them views, likes and acclaim

So, they can sustain

Take lessons from NRI's how to praise the nation

They are the true study of perfection

Don't take anything as a criticism

It's a time of absolute despotism!

On this last point I finish my submission;

Now that there is someone trying to find a new version

Based upon facts with a mission

I admire that beacon

Coz I don't want to reckon

I eat the fruit of professorship

Open my eyes and sit every morning for worship!

———— • ★ • ————

POLLUTANT

I have a plumeria flower plant in my garden

Like in the lawns of nobles

A symbol of worship

In the form of deity!

That provides tranquility seizing the discord of vanity

I breathe in the fragrance

And breathe out the essence

I devour the reflection

To stop the decay of my inner self

Presenting myself in a finer shelf;

I learn ...

How to dig and till soil in the garden

I too watch ...

How plantation can be done by the stardom

Not to get get fruits out of that

But to spread oxygen

Instead of explosive nitrogen

To escalate in the hemisphere

To protect the air which is polluting social media atmosphere!

———— • ★ • ————

SCENARIO

Buy a true picture!

Not mine

Rather what I have painted

Not from colours

Instead from pencil

It's a scene on white paper

In a sunflower type rapper

It's a vocal thing

Comes out like a spring

It's a precise and vivid image

Neither to complicate

Nor to decorate

It's a scenario

In a clear and sharp language

I am presenting here a teaser

You all can buy it!

It's a time to crave

It's a time to be brave

Become a little classic

Become a bit restless

To pull yourself out of threat!

———————— • ★ • ————————

NOT MY TASK!

It was not my task

But I am writing down

That was not my path

Even though I am walking around

To engrave the foot print

Not on sand

Not on wind

To make a wave

That can wash the filth;

My journey is to melt the cloud

To turn into water in it's true shape

Thereby we can see the sky

In true colour like peerless lake

To behold **ALPHABETS** over and over again

To encourage to read, to write, to speak

That too without any strain!

———— •★• ————

TRANSITION

Take out the veneer of dust

From the sunlight

Come out of the void

Behave like wind allowing self to ventilate

Keep on sipping water at certain intervals

Permitting voices to remain wet and curl

Proclaim what you want to be done

Let the channel appear green

Never eject it to succumb

No need to enact wisdom in guise

There is no such thing one can hide

Gift fragrant flowers to sightless

Present vibrating tone to deaf

Embrace the violent souls

To turn them into gold

Such sort of transition is required

If you don't possess analogous equations

Try to hire!

———————— • ★ • ————————

I AM HERE!

Suddenly light was gone

And I felt like thunder storm

Was unable to touch the silhouette

My eyes were muffed and heart puffed

Looking for rays from the defunct stars

Swiftly moon whispered

I am here!

I am here!

For your repair!

Change the words for the betterment of whole

Reconcile with the soul

All together kick the stuff that hurts

Pray a bit!

Once again you will be hit!

City is like a nursing home

Someone walking wearing a mask

Another one is hiding the head

In a manner surgeon do in the OT bed

Population is in mode of absolute personal care

Students are anxious to turn around the table

By reconstructing future comparatively fair

Oh! hike in fees put them in despair

One judgment is out

Majority is so proud

Minority can't shout

Now my head is churning

After doing this tuning

Now it's your turn to switch on the radio

I am hankering to listen some music

Of your kudo!

———————— •★• ————————

RESCUE

Become so much than yourself

Delay all the days

Work is more and time is less

You can't afford to rest

Rescue nation in the night

Also repeat the same in the bright light

Widen the road, make it broad

Stay Awake!

Whosoever you meet on the way

Find out the meaning of every sentence in length

To embrace yourself with strength

Don't except the lollipop that spreads scent

Take a little pain to draw sense

On the outline of your nation's atlas

Love the plain paper

Rather than newspaper

Express your views on it

Suffocate less!

And breathe more!

At least the air is still free!

Thank God!

———————— •★• ————————

THE EXTRAORDINARY PERSON

The Extraordinary Person, one in billion

Is ready to give lecture

Ready to be closer to the picture

Picture of peace vs. violence

It's time to clean your ears

By hearing words that don't fear

Words that don't yell

Reminding you that silence is hell

When there is need to utter feelings

When we strive to get healings

Be ready to listen

If not live

Surf the YouTube in the kitchen

To cook a new vision

We ought to be supple enough

While hearing to both the versions

Of rampage vs. pacifism

In universities as well as in auditoriums

Get yourself altered

From the Extraordinary Person who is a tailor

Tailor of knowledge

Who stitches dresses for your mind

And prays!

May your attention shine!

Education should remain the prime focus

Never say Gandhi was bogus

Collect some accessories for your dress

Put it on your clothing and press

The Extraordinary Person is a costumier

For the best fittings

Look up to him

Here you go!

And listen to his lecture!

———————— • ★ • ————————

SHADOW

Sea is annexed and separated from the shore

Water runs to and fro

Neither dust nor fire

In a soft attire

That is the place I desire;

Dry leaves shredded on the long roads

I can watch the shadow crossing the corridor

Holding in one hand are the memoirs

And the eyes recollecting the chronicles of grappling with the bonfire

Gathering the courage and lightening the future

Such lidless eyes I desire!

Oh! Don't get confused

Stroll towards the roof

There you will find one individual

In the form of university, clearly visible

Tomb like rooms

Library that blooms

Flowers are the students

Preparing themselves to spread perfumes of

revolutions, renaissance and evolutions;

For such view

You all should desire!

What will you do?

Without any such progressive clue

Charismatic glue!

Morning dew!

———————— • ★ • ————————

TRANSCRIPT

I observed the projector and slides

Time after time

One picture then eight lines

Battle is going on

Between the strong and the fraud

Basis are the facts, reports, videos

To intersect the baseless theories also their promos;

This man is standing with whom?

Lector points out looking at

the cut out of a chieftain and a troll

Such are the lines that rock & roll

Amongst pupils sitting in the conference hall

Praise the abuse

Say great! It's lovely!

In the times of googly!

Winter has creeped in

Disorientation of the earth from the sun is apparent

You can easily claim that's nature's coherent

Do not do hustle-and-bustle for light

Stay in a mode of good night

Your head is already covered with a thick sheet

Thus no one can see your deeds

Make an assertion!

You are certain a historian!

Your stuff can be spread dangerously via IT cell in the name of Hooghly!

Yeah!

I feed you with "Sarcasm Culture"

To save your brain from the damage of "Parahippocampal Gyrus";

Now my presentation is all yours

I couldn't sleep whole night

Just to hold the flashlight

To bring you all on the shores

And don't transmit it in crores!

— • ★ • —

ULTIMATE

Vomit all the injected poisonous substances from your
skull
Prove them null
No angel is going to arrive for your rescue
You have to draw your own avenue
For a better future;

Stop struggling in your father's lap
You are aged enough to take a step
Towards the shower
Towards the tower
Of Hope!
Without tying yourself to the rope
For a better future;

Sleep in the earth
To submerge your fears in the dust
You may feel enchanted

After groping the compactness of the molecules

And automatically your hands will speak

For a better future;

When applause break out before entering the room

Atmosphere gets bloomed

Prolonged standing ovation mixed with infectious aura in

a forum not in opera

Your fumes in the brain get settled

Just by hearing the expound

For a better future!

———————— • ★ • ————————

TYPEWRITER

The age of which is gone though

But I want to use Typewriter

Where I can type humanism

Can write evidences over dogma

Can elaborate the scene without the cover of spectre on

the head

At a normal pace

In very much solace;

I want to do mastery in Orthography

Excelling in spelling, punctuation, emphasis etc.

In my free time

Where I can borrow alphabets

From it's original language

And script them in cursive letters

Focusing on critical writing

Unescorted by biting;

I want to do Printing through an inked ribbon

Using phonemes between slashes

And reviving the era of angel brackets

Enduring the legacy of past type settings

And too with a cause

Where newspapers do not spread fraud;

I want to type manuscript

To do original composing for the publication

Also, one to submit in library

As a document before getting printed

To ensure it does not get edited

By the system via scissors type of edges!

———————— • ✦ • ————————

PLANTATION

O citizens! plant a tree of democracy

In your lawns

In the balcony in a pot

And watch every day how it grows

Water it daily with your thoughts

Via reading periodicals roam in all the directions

Left, Right & Centre!

Feed them with manure at certain intervals

And only the bio one made up of informations

Not the chemicals which exists in the form of news

channels

In each and every home

They are the pest in the guise of the best

You will find the plant growing transparent and vibrant

After the rain

You can reach the autumn without flooding in the drain

You may smell calm, colourful beautiful flower

At your doorstep

Spreading light of unity, primacy of wisdom making you de-stress

By side you can lean on the chair

Your hands can touch it's flair

Now you will find yourself a transformed person

You can park your car in an allotted dimension

In a perfect citizenry accommodation!

———————— • ★ • ————————

MARCH

I do not unearth anyone

I only expose my knowledge

Offer that in a plate

Bare like a slate Free of cost

Whosoever wants are free to take a glimpse, a bite

Get guide to ride!

When I speak it means-

I am out of the envelope now

I do not expect everyone to bow

Just keep your ears open

Just unbolt the window of your head

I also do so

As and when I listen to the people in a row

All should remain compact and visible

Amongst the multitude

With a sense of latitude

Make the banners your voice

Flag them high

In the case nobody gives ear

In the times of denial

Come on the resistance movement

March, March and March!

———————— • ★ • ————————

VOYAGE

Fearless voyage is on at the parapets

To guard the constitution setting the daring eyes

On every nook and corner at the same time

Rocks, rivers, sea, tree ...

A single name cried by the jamboree

We all can see the journey of that canoe

Anchored and sailing close by

Higher on all the sides, flag is flung

Crossing the surf carrying slices of fun

That's not a fight

It's a journey to overcome which is not right

Pier is waiting

Not one who is floating

This is the beauty of this fearless voyage

Can't we all board such canoe?

———————— • ★ • ————————

SPEAK

Allow the words to come out

The words which are echoing

In the world inside you;

In the land of darkness

Spread the light

One within

And one outside;

Present is the time

Don't wait for any other rhyme

Your shadow is your chime

Walk alongside of your steps

Keep on transiting between the silence and the soliloquy

Your shaken voice will certainly find reply;

In the land of cactus

Trust your shadow behind you

Create a plasma globe inside you

Filled with noble gasses

Let the fluorescent colours glow

Let them flow;

Tell your eyes to reappear

To read

Tell your ears to rehear

To listen

To the works of ethicists

Whether it is Gandhi, John Stuart Mill or Charles Darwin!

———— • ★ • ————

NOTABLE

System is hiding the real tableau

Audiences are unable to take the view,

Television anchors have left shoe leather reporting

They no more crave for news gatherings

Sound alike boo-boo boomer

Always ready to hit the hammer

Studio debates are ultimate visions

Name them as hellion, dragons, demons

They enact equal to villains;

Only a few historians are ready to pen

About this weakened realm

The strongest medium of awakening

Is in the process of shrinking

Learn only to bow in the feet of the tycoon

Sensex too is rolling falling from the moon;

Minster is traveling to offer prayer

On the delivery of raffles which is a part of warfare

ISRO launch of Mars Orbiter Mission

Spending millions of dollars on it, is not a fun

Such episodes are now very common

We love to play the game of mammon;

Upper side of the body is empty

Of the larger population in plenty

Culture of reasoning brain has been drained

What is left behind is only frame

Unwritten things are in volumes

Those who can write making vacuums

Ghost of fear bumming around citizens

I'm mentioning these confusions

To bring you out from illusions;

Remain happy in your spaces!

Don't forget to offer Rosogolla to goddess!

––––––– • ★ • –––––––

REVISED BILL

There was a live lesson telecasted for bird brained people boldly

Crawlers whispered o really!

Although a few couldn't digest in their bellies

They decided that it's better to keep quiet

Howbeit, their minds broke and remained attentive to such recite;

So what is it ?

Voice ....

1. What is going on is perilous
2. Now it's a law
3. If someone tries to criticise will be called malicious
4. Don't try to be hilarious
5. Gas chamber is not a word to rehearse
6. It's a curse
7. What happened is another step for the elimination of undesirable
8. Gait to create pain that will remain unbearable
9. Gandhi's picture is fading
10. His soul is shaking

11. Time of taking two minutes selfies coming to an end

12. Old Constitution may no more be in trend

13. Pages are replaced

14. So, get ready to be in a cage

15. Commissions are steady with the clean chits

16. A particular religion is in fits

17. CAB and NRC are now best friends

18. Well there are pictures of celebrating hands

19. Where you can't even find internet connection in 5000 bucks

20. Oh, Wow that sucks!

———————— • ★ • ————————

NOTHING

He is nothing

Like a common man

He is universal

Blear eyes, sore face, bare feet

Puzzled most of the time

Not very clear

Even in his shrine;

He is nothing

Lacks words for narration

He has appetite for adventure

His eyes craves for details

Finds it impossible to cross the bridge

To meet the audiences

Coz neither he is literary nor popular;

He is nothing

He paddles cycle

His eyes sets on motorcycle

But his pocket can't buy

He has never ever received meed of admiration

At every nook and corner, he is shun;

He is nothing

He is a chap that shrinks

He laughs and flouts when in chafe

Never travelled to New York to visit "Birch Coffee cafe"

When finds money he drinks beer

Can't even write a single line

All the time smears in fears;

He is nothing

He is a poor dull man as if toy

Nobody calls him Sir!

Though his family always wanted him to be named as

Viceroy!

Have at any time he performed the best?

The answer is No! No! No!

And too in a row;

He is nothing

He does nothing

His clock is always slow

His copy is empty

His is totally "Humpty Dumpty"

Short and fat!

Needs to pull the stool
To touch the rack!

You are nothing!
Hey!
Hello!
I am talking about you!
Can you hear me!
You are a common man!
You live in my body and brain!

———— • ★ • ————

DEMONSTRATION

A) Public

1) This land is for everyone. We believe in equality in the nation among all civilian.

2) We do not want to be seen as a data encrypted on paper. Rather as a living human being and a breathing citizen charter.

3) Don't try to be tricky like Trump. Do not expect us to be dumb and numb .

4) Now we know you. In return we want you to understand us too.

5) Stop the exercise of dividing people. We all are friends. No need to make skeptical trends.

6) We voted for you. We only can be the reason to throw you out to the place you belong to.

7) Keep your single colour in your mantel. We believe in shining like rainbows in the sky channel.

B) Power

1) In speech -I am with you. Trust me. We all are one. Me and you.

2) In the House- All the amendments are in your favour. Not like the previous government for vote bank politics to shimmer.

3) Internet is shut only as a precautionary measure. Feel pleasure!

4) Opposition is misleading the population. Raising the posters "Unity is our Mission"!

5) Right of each and every citizen is intact. As a matter of fact.

6) Police is for your protection. Don't harm the public property. Don't jumble with the authority.

7) You all directly can give the suggestion instead of doing procession

Note-

What is missing are the table and chairs!

Dialogue and communication between the two layers!

———— • ★ • ————

THE PROMISE OF THE LIPS

To trust or to distrust thee?
Answer to this question in hints
As he makes promises from the lips;
Burning cars, bloody noses,
weeping father, dead body in mortuary
waiting for justice
Helpless you and me
Country is looking for peace;

There we find no snow on the Christmas tree
Some drops vaporised
Some dismissed
Moving to and fro to catch the visual of light in plea;
Temperature has reached above the "Arctic Circle"
Either
Burn your clothes
Or-
Burn your houses
To catch the attention of fourth pole
For sure it's going to give your voices a hole;

15 lakhs and a new year!

Why to fear?

Check your bank balance in a hypnotised stance

You may get it by chance

To celebrate New Year in tips

Since you have with you –

"The Promises of the Lips "!

———————— • ★ • ————————

SMELL OF ARMPITS

If you require to know the ground realities

Smell the armpits!

Armpits of the farmers

Armpits of the labourers

Armpits of the students

Armpits of all of them

Stinking with the sweat

Dirty and wet

Enter in the herd

In guise of the bird

Then one by one sit on their shoulders

Get the real taste of the blunders

Made by the voters

By pushing wrong button under the shutters

Now they all are protesting

To get back their casting

But it's difficult

Thus, keep on smelling

Until it reaches to the kingdom

And they start yelling in dusk and dawn

Stop it!

I am ready to repair!

I am ready to do shampoo on your hair

I am coming with the towel

To wipe your sweat

And too with a spray of fragrance

Now I can sense your patience

Beyond imagination

For the sake of my "Nose"

On the atlas of the globe!

Your "Smell of the Armpits" have proved

We call the largest democracy

You proved!

————— •★• —————

STRUGGLE OF A ZERO

O God!

Have mercy on my head

For I am zero

I want to bang it on the door

And also, on a sea shore

I get crazy

I get messy

When I throw the words

Useless

Uncounted

Unaccounted

Half bare & half clothed

Demon dig me like a bore

I am a dried man on a wet land

Please make me a CLORE!

Please make me a CLORE!

———— •★• ————

REBEL VIA ART

I am stating the truth!

"Take it or leave it" aspect of journalism is no more vital

Fake is pivotal, slip-ups are inevitable

Extremely tight deadlines take the media to shrines

Some also travel to search ghosts in the mines;

Physical fitness have become the best version of newsy
agents

Of course they don't live in tents

Super cars, plush bungalows, best social connections are
there strengths

And are much loved spokesperson to their statesman
friends;

Wow! Television Rating Points (TRP) passes great vibes

To those who love flights

Please! Let's go back to 20th century

Only avant-garde and modernist poets can save us from
going to mortuary

Through digging our suppression

Bringing out of our aggression instead

Paving way towards making country a man's land

As good as it looks in a map on stand;

We may rebel via art

Never mind if we don't get a cart

To present pictures of heart

To capture lives

To mend the discord spread by lies!

———————— • ★ • ————————

SOUL - SEARCH

People are lacking the soul

And poets are facing a shortfall

Of old skill of writing as a whole

Incomplete are the verse

Tongues are covered with masks so can't utter

That's the biggest curse;

O shucks! Writer's lyrics are in accordance with the superior's views

Singers are re-mixing their tunes

Nothing new is emerging

Gandhiji's ideology is immersing;

Solution-

Bathe in fire, water and air which are the elements of life

To get yourself purify

Valiant force joins in this course

Providing a subtle picture of cure

All the viruses of ignorance starts crawling

Resulting in the character's overhauling;

A book has waltzed in me

Through my eyes into brain

And thus, I feel less strained

While I read it, words travel downwards

Then comes out of my fingers

A scene triggers, I get my gestures;

I pass this to everybody

Am in a no mood to get aristocracy

Only to say remember

We all are super animals

There should be no game of numbers

Documenting is a crazy act

We all are nosy, bewildered, that's the fact!

———————— • ★ • ————————

HAIL - HAIL

Night sedated me with the sleep

I slept deep

I left behind everything

After the day of ting-bing,

In between I saw a dream

Of pink flower and a beam,

I followed the light whole night

I heard the sound of lecture

To repair my fracture

To come out of the turmoil

I too called a name to sail

In a peaceful rail

Here there were no hospitals and wards

No fear of corona war

Neither of face identifications and software car

Totally free from veil

With naked thoughts of zeal

I recommend everyone to have such voyage

Where you are only with you

In a fearless attire!

———————— • ★ • ————————

TEA - MEDITATION

Sips of morning tea takes on a trip of passion

An aroma of peace fills the erosion

Ship starts sailing

In the scene which is prevailing

My world releases

Blossoms towards increases

Some four books, two spectacles,

Does miracles

Feelings becomes soft and smiles

This juncture maintains a distinctive height

To combat with the flying flight

Oneness of heaven and earth shines

All the curses go down

Life reappears with a crown

I take an opportunity to thank

Once again to my "Proper Noun"!

———— • ★ • ————

CHOOSE YOUR TIME!

While affluent came out yawning from their blankets

Daily wages workers are stranded on roads absent

mattresses

Without money, food and transport, still life is on board

Walking, walking and walking

No one is talking

To save the energy that will take them to the shores;

Everyone is catching, watching these heartfelt images

Though feeling scary to touch the real sketches

Life is turning vinegar and salt

A pinch is enough to say halt

I can't do a bit of mine

Because i am stuck in a shrine with a duty

To look after an angel

Unable to move whatever may be the angle;

But you all.......

After a hiatus when everybody will

come together again

You will be asked -

What you did?

Where were you?

How you contributed?

Did you come forward?

Why you were a coward?

When the humanity was in strains;

So be ready for such questionnaire while showing off your
garb

It's not a joke

Virus is crushing us like we are under a big rock

Virus of gap, between the poor and the hap is now
revealing

Nature has stolen the clothes

To bare the hoax

Be ready to see!

To judge!

To do!

Time has come

To mend humanity via resurrection;

Better choose your time to start....

Whether it is one, three or four o'clock

But remember one thing time is over of convenience!

———————— • ★ • ————————

DOCTOR

Morning-

Hello, Hello -The Doctor said!

He greets the patient wearing the mask

Not scared of the image that is dark

He showered all his energies to perform the task

He is young, bearded, slogged

All the time ready to fight

In the manner best and right;

Oh, No - Doctor's colleague said!

You too have high temperature!

Please lie down on bed!

Sister! Sister! Put the oxygen cylinder on

That means he too is infected while fighting syndrome

And one more addition in the isolation zone;

Scarcity of PPE (Personal Protective Equipment) is

hurting

To the sisters who are trained in tackling pain

To the doctors who are struggling to cope up with strain

Waiting for someone to raise their voice

About safety and understanding their difficulties in the

loop of vent & void;

Night-

Suddenly a scene appears to knock the door of

governance

In a shape of comparative guild

Starts the Local v/s Abroad drill

Questions start dropping

Screen started popping

One by one to show what's going on there and here

Regarding hospital ambulance and it's all gears

Test kits, PPE and all other fears

Bottom line is to depict the realistic figures

By way of putting pressure

In a thorough procedure

As an effort to get control of Virus Flare-up!

DING - DONG

Everybody is singing the same song

Stay home putting aside qualm

With your loved ones doing ting tong

All of a sudden-

All humans are prisoned

All birds are freed

Globe is bobbing

Movement of latitude and longitude is throbbing

Studio has turned into room

Hanging pictures describing the bloom

Gestures are less than before

Though eyes are same touching the shore;

In this blind time, I make an appeal-

Love the air

Praise the sound of cuckoos

Enjoy the dance of peacocks

For some time forget the pulses and rice

Just think about mice

How they run

When they do not get ration!

———————— • ★ • ————————

INTELLIGENCE

I listen whole day but still craving

To hear something engraving

Pure, wise and containing soft curls

What I heard....

There it is nothing about pearls

Say, Fear, Populace, Solace are some of the words;

Different sort of survival you find

In the writing which starts from the road

And goes till the bathroom and also to the shrine

Rama, Gandhi, Gauri, Obama

All names get a place and that's fine;

And I have seen people briefing

After thorough reading that -

"yeah I have got a clarity of thought"!

"Must read for those who doesn't have hope from the Rose!"

"This will help you from passing through chilly

nightmare and will take you to fresh morning breeze"!

At the end, gist is this....

What we see is nothing but cruel

You still have to struggle to make the country beautiful!

————— •★• —————

SILHOUETTES

In the moon light

Black flowers turn white

Blue water becomes the mirror of this sight

Two silhouettes start dancing

In such heavenly night

Traveling and meeting each other

On silver wireless line

Exchanging the notes of heart

But without the beat

Not to disturb people in the sleep

Night passes by

And again, time to say good bye

For the next day

Hoping that sun will spread the light

To make their love more bright

More clear, though less in the people's eyes!

--- ⋅★⋅ ---

CONFESSION

Yeah, I confess! I am in Love!

With the Eyes

With the Nose

With the Lips

With the palm and fingers

With the toes tied with the slippers

With the Sassy thoughts 💭

With the whole you

As you Are

Yes, I Confess!

———————— • ★ • ————————

FIREWORK

Cracker work are not allowed in the space

Since pollution is creating menace

Let's do firework with you babe

Will light the day like beacon hurricane

In your arms as if insane

My soul will slip and travel to your heart

Making from two to one all of a sudden

Bringing love out of the blue nature's game

Lottery should not go in vain

Taste and smell of skin may travel to origin

From where it started to meet the bundane

Will you lit the lamp with your passionate hand ?

Putting aside the frame and shape of rumination

You know passion do not believe in examination

Showers, thunders be back

Sing the same music on the same track

Free yourself from words and shake

Calm, controlled, soothing belle

Let's do firework with you babe !

———— • ★ • ————

PIOUS TIME

Silence breaks itself in the night

And travels to meet the craving soul

Which waits with the open eyes

Sometime gazing sky and sometimes stars

In this pious time there is no one to make pejorative

insinuation

Road is clear to travel to the destination

Where soul press itself to the soul

Melting the beats of hearts, of course

In the breeze of mind, the lover shines

Like diamonds light

Like rainbow in the sky

Slowly they closes eyes to sleep and dream

One more dream for the day next

What they are going to text

Again, the same soulful songs

Dancing words without drums

With singing hands

That are blessed with the pens

With tender moving fingers

Pouring the words

Mixed with blood

Feelings are such

Dreams & Real will move together

With hands in hands

Loving and kissing their palms

Beginning of the story is this

We may see the climax

When it fix!

———————— •★• ————————

LUCID

Unseen existence of warmth trembles and shakes

With the leaves like flakes

No vapour breathe on the solid surface remains

As the fog fades

Ocean and sky are only expressions of brains

In factual and real

Sphere and stratosphere both are insane!

———————— •★• ————————

PAVE YOUR WAY

Light a lamp in the midnight

Start walking towards the grave

Who are dead still brave

Sacrificed there lives to broaden way

Not of the roadway but of brain

Instances are many ....

Like Mother and APJ

Then start your journey in a new way

Serve the nature, feed the beggar, raise voice with
articulation

In form of poems and prose

If this can be your course

Cross the hurdles that comes your way

This is not the reply to your question anyway

Words aren't enough I just mean to say

Everyone must do there duties

In some or the other physical way

Hopes and rays will surely enlighten narrow pathway

That's the demand of today!

———————— • ★ • ————————

CLIMATE

My search for climate is over

I feel empowered

I possess cold breeze

And my thoughts never freeze

Makes me feel alive

It's wavy, soft, free, naive

Now I can travel miles and miles

Without stepping out for office

I can disburse so many files

My vehicle is opaque

Nobody can overtake

Also, I do not need brake

This journey is like a cake

Sweet, brown, engraved name with a paste

Angel cuts and I get a taste

No bets, no threats

Everything is safe

Covered though face to face

This climate is my only solace!

————— • ★ • —————

DOSE FOR HEALTH

Nothing gratifies more than hearing rational discourse

Free from hate and chaos

Which can be collected in a cup

And then just sup

Here sup doesn't stand for What's up?

It comes in a form of medicine to cure the humanness

Which is getting infected like an abscess

Contaminated and have elements of hatred

And thread of disbelief and rumours

Dipped in diseased humours

Where identity has come under threat;

In such current times ....

There is a single screen on hub

For orating "Best Practice" on prime orb

With all the natural ingredients in it

To cure this pandemic!

———————— • ★ • ————————

PEDAGOGY

There is one presentation paper

Which I have prescribed for myself

It's not a docility

Neither it's velocity

It's a curiosity

With a pace!

Of the phase!

On the space!

No race!

No chase!

That will take me to my destination

In a slow motion

Now I would like to make revelation-

It's a pedagogy

Of being you in me

And the universe begins teaching

And cultivating my upper hill!

———— • ★ • ————

COUNTRY'S TALK

The meticulous reports on Covid-19 presentation gives
shock, strain and pressure
And there is a talk to measure;

The scene is such -
Angry, hungry are wandering
Impatient to reach their native places
No travel means have been provided
Amid the lockdown crisis
So, they decided
To go by foot without any hood
Scorching heat and no food
Numbers are in thousands
All of them are labourers
Other modes are cycles and trolly
Also, some are shaking in tractors;

Pregnant women are too walking
One has delivered baby on highway
This is not any sort of a road show by the way

Whether it is Bhopal, chattisgarh,
Delhi, Mumbai, UP's Agra or Bihar
Videos are disturbing
System is churning;

Some of the tired walkers slept on the railway track
Crushed by the freight train
Dead bodies got packed in sacks
Eventually reached homes
In coffin packs
Some met with mishaps
No problems!
There is one class which is busy with hip hops!

Reasons of struggle for going back are many -
No work
No money
No ration
Only disquisition and oration!
Tenants are under stress
To pay the rent

Poignant are the visuals
In any situation they are not ready to wait in the hustle
Feeling dumped by the state
They are in complete haste;

Coupons have been distributed

But ration is muted

Middle class has too joined the line

To get free wheat,pulse and rice

Even if you are technology illiterate

For everything online registration is a must

No option left but to trust;

An example of government's tyranny can be seen

System is not keen

To ease the pain

They only believe in bullet train!

———————— • ★ • ————————

ORIGIN

As long as time will stay in our lives

Let these pictures witness the distress

For the years to come

That how the poor migrants left in the lurch

And the government didn't do much

Suddenly everything took away from them

They walked alone from the realm

On the unknown path

Carrying the load of wrath;

Till they stayed in the metropolitans

Gave themselves nothing

And the cities were watching

Now taking back with them -

Boils on the feet

Scorching heat

Only biscuits to eat

Nobody knew their names

Until they were smashed by the trucks and train;

Secretly started their journey

Some returned to their desired land

With weeping hands

Want to work again

But only in their own lands;

Skies and earth are happy

At least they know the truth

Of the fake city lites

What we call them smart cities of heights!

———— •★• ————

SIDE EFFECTS

When the system dehydrated

Poor suffocated

Beaten with sticks

To break their ribs

Settlers relied on a few

Who joined them with a media crew

Narrated their agony

How five-kilogram grain is not enough

Life is getting beyond tough

Weather is also rough

Companies are closed in tuff

Meals & breakfast can only be seen on hashtags

Ladies are no more symbol of sacred lotus

Sitting in circles

Evidently as turtles

Waiting with a bag for meagre food allocation

In so many locations

What kind of justice is this?

No king ruled like hiss!

Is this a state or a dynasty?

Eight crores is not a less number

Of city labourers

But real figures of migrants getaway are hiding in a

tumbler

Though thousand rail started

Still people on station bombarded

Now they have explored ways which are more desolate

To make themselves isolate;

Children are riding bicycles to help mummy-pappa

In getting out of this cuppa

Of diseased voyage

Covid is nothing in front of governance breakage

Thank God!

Mother "Yamuna" is fulfilling friendship

Her shores have always been their flagship

Certainly, they will cross the borders

In the absence of orders!

This was the transmitted story

Part of a chronicle theory

Of lockdown side effects puree!

———————— • ★ • ————————

DAILY DOCUMENTATION

The rush of desperate displaced people is such

That nobody can blush

"We want to die on our own land!"

"We don't need food!"

"Don't ask about our problems,

take out copy and pen and you would be tired of writing!"

Disbelief, tears and agony

Voices are many

No end of woes

Vignettes are in a rows;

Suddenly a man appears on the Television screen

Address social themes

Takes his seat at six 'o clock

On the back side we may see books in flocks

Clearly explains the covid-19 current scenario –

-Dignity of the daily wagers have been squashed

-Seemingly their basic human rights are thrashed

-No slot of compassion can be find

-Press conferences suspended

-Number of the patients escalated

-Press releases are coming in print

-Information is blinking

-Reviews are shrinking;

Moreover-

Mismanagement is in focus

Government proves to be bogus

New identity has been stamped

Registered & Non-Registered!

Is a new poster on the state land

Lack of synergy between the states hurts

Some of the workers are without shirts;

Contrary to the unrest

Some are passing on their best

By way of distributing food, water along with good wishes

It proves humanity is not dead

We can always improve the conditions

To show the throne their bones

Because we are not stones!

———————— • ★ • ————————

PROLOGUE

There is no dearth of words on the earth

Yet in sentences we don't see any word

Hence, they are not worth

Media is now wordless

There meanings are hopeless

No words!

So, no compassion!

Therefore, no picture of comfort!

Expressions are in chains

Only a few words left to describe pains

Humanity needs to be pulled out by cranes

From all the so-called strata of the society

Covered in the fallacious identity;

Mr Sound Recordist!

Are you ready?

Light, Camera, Real!

Sound Recordist-Action or Real!

Director- Real Action and will wait for the reactions

Test of patience starts now

Not to say wow

Time has come to bow

Watching their ignominy

Here comes the symphony

Of sync sound

Minimal edited footage which shall speak loud;

Mr Cameraman cranked the camcorder-

Scene comes in long shot

Masks covering the face tops

Walking silently and slowly

With bottle and a pithu bag

Filled with their own versions of strife

Direct cinema of life

Stepping energy less

Crossing the city that has become loveless

Labourers feet zoomed

Camera bloomed

Capturing silence and whispers of sorrow

They are marked irrelevant even to borrow;

Tooting sound of passing motors

But where is the reporter?

Yeah yeah he is there!

Traveller-"I am going from Dharavi to East Champaran Bihar"

"At the back there is no way thus I can't stay like stray "

"Nobody asked for food "

"Though everyone knew we were staying under the roof hungry and penniless "

Picture continues-

Spotless submissions, No views;

Another location with another tale

Be ready with the handkerchief to

wipe away your tear rail

Young man paddling the rickshaw

Please note down that I am only explaining the sequence in a row

I am not George Bernard Shaw

Again, reel zoomed!

Karrr....karrr

Three children and three adults

Again, reporter uttered-

From where are you coming?

Coming from Ghaziabad he answered

Pulling, pulling and pulling

Ache of hundreds of kilometres is running

Four days of journey already covered

He is one who has lost his job of shepherd;

These are not only two scenes

Wide open your pulpy eyes and gaze them till the end

Until you can bear!

———————— • ★ • ————————

SHORT TRIP TO THE LEGACY OF NEHRU

Doors daily opens with the ringing of bell

Good great ambience of sprawling lawn spreads spell

Yes, it's TEEN MURTI BHAVAN

Build in nineteen thirty

Official residence of first Prime Minister of India

Mr Jawahar Lal Nehru

Hero of hope and despair!

Hero of praise and criticism!

Always remained flair

Everyday around three thousand people come here to go through

To teach themselves history

Build in approx forty-four acres beautiful land territory

Present is going to describe the history on his 125th birth anniversary

Immediately got connected with the old trees

Recalling studies of student life in the library

Three tall statues got installed in the year nineteen twenty-two

And are momentous of Hyderabad,Mysore and Jodhpur's lancers crew

Here Patel use to walk down to have talks with Nehru

Totally opposite of today's Watsap reviews

Present has obtained adequate permissions for camera take

To go inside

With a professor as a guide

Firstly, we may see Gandhi movie filming site

To get memoir insight

Present and the history are in even frames

Both are lonesome, without stains

Nehru's childhood was princely

But his life was hurly-burly

Spent 1170 days in jail

To get the British rule derail

While studying in London he started bending towards right

Attracted by Tilak and Lala Lajpat Rai's philosophy which matters

Had regular conversations with Gandhi via letters

That describes fundamental variance of opinions between the two

So many snaps fixed on the walls

A legacy which is so tall

One wall hanging attracts more

"Papu's " letters to his daughter from prison

We can catch them in publication

Compiled in shape of a configuration book "Glimpses of World History"

In it chapters are many, this is only a summary

Nehru's slogan of "Complete Independence" backed by Gandhi

Being aggressive he spoke of element of boycott of English Rule

Remained vocal in front of his father

Criticised his "Dominion Status" bluntly

Surfacing their political differences clearly

Now comes the replica train

Which covered last journey of his mortal remains

His quote has been plagiarised

But he is not here to fight

Neither anybody is doing so

This is the plight!

Please note it down -

A peacock is the witness of half of this compact trip

Who resides in the lawns

And all I have taken this from YouTube atheneum !

———————— • ★ • ————————

JOURNEY OF MIGRANTS

Trains are getting late and late

Of the migrants

Who churned their spines to make our apartments

No food distributed to save their fate

And where it is given, smelly and stale

Dry throat and thirst for water

All the scenes are of hunger

Audiences will you please watch some real stories-

01897 is the train number

Started on 23/05/2020 from Mumbai to Chapra

After moving for certain yards

Started traveling backwards

Towards Mughalsarai

May be in search for some Sarai!

For shelter!

Everybody was crying water, water!

In the temperature around 47degree celsius not less than laceration

And again goes back to Samastipur to it's final destination

Passengers were given single packet of food

In the days of journey which was so rude;

Another "Labourers Special Rail"started from Surat

Took four to five days to reach Siwan

In between moved to and fro

You may call it tram!

Halting and moving!

Again, halting and moving!

Travelled rather roamed to so many unwanted stations

This is not a mock

We have live testimony of "Jane Aalam"on record

In five days only a platter of five breads and pickle served

To feed their belly which was curbed

On one more day they received some dry meal packet

Which was again difficult to digest

Five lakh passengers did not even get water

No words left to state this disaster;

But Mr Minister is not ready to tweet this folly

Must be doing Rolly-Polly!

This should have been like this –

"We apologise for distributing only 84 lakh food packets
instead of 98."

"And I have ordered for the strictest action and to pay
damages ".

These are not merely stories or accounts

Height of shame and humiliation one can count

Officers! Take out one register

Make a list and tick

And relish your breakfast with knife and pan

After looking at this train clan!

———— •★• ————

THE LOTTERY

Without even buying a ticket
From any ticket gallery
I have won a lottery;

This lottery is designed in a special tray
It showcases roses and pearls all the way
It plays a significant part in my life
Raises me to a family of highest crest
Something which is beyond zest;

It's not like colonial types
It's also not to sponsor war hypes
Neither to get prize items such as crockery
Nor in shape of failed "Mount Road Lottery"
Rather it brings unusual aroma in frequency
Carrying a soothing love of decency;

It can also be named as lotto

And that's the expanse where I glow

After watching the flair of intelligence

To kiss the florescence

To touch the gift of benevolence!

———————— • ★ • ————————

HE

The narrow lane, the wide lane

Long roads, the highways

My January, my December

All the seconds, all the hours

My time, my power

Tap and shower

And between A to Z

R is exclusive

As it brings rains

On the dried thoughts and planes

Anything you can name on the universe

Is He!

———— • ★ • ————

JAIL

Squirrel that goes up and down

Down and up whole day on the wall of my nest

Reminds all the time of my restlessness

I can vouch

I am the witness

Of restlessness of that living being

It can be put other way

She enacts me

When I am at my place

She and I both are same

In a very different way

We both are living creatures

Struggling to get peace

In the world that is sleaze

Time and space is squeezed

Heart is far away from man

And man lives in pram

Always shouts in poise

To stay away from raising voice

In such times squirrel takes rides

And I write watching her shakes

In my brakes

Thinking of you, how to woo

When everything is blue

Now squirrel has crossed the ladder

She is now on the roof

No more in my sight

But I am still sitting there

Looking at you in my paper

All the time in the nature

That allows me to meet you

In such a manner

In a calm and cool weather

No complaints, no regrets

With trees, air and water

Until these are my friends

Our love will remain unharmed

How much harsh may be the scratcher!

———— • ★ • ————

DADDY

Daddy! Daddy!

I cried!

He was in coma

Next day again I moaned, Daddy!

No reply

He was in deep sleep

On all the other coming days

I screamed

can you hear me?

One day his lashes mumbled softly

In a consoling like whisper

Very next evening again I whimpered

Daddy! Daddy!

He was motionless in the hospital bed

And started shivering in my soul and body

Shaking me to come back

And to say Good -Bye!

———— •★• ————